I0528113

THIS CAN'T BE REALITY

A memoir through love and loss by
Jimilyn Smith Kell

Edited by Denice Todd Hubbard

These memories have been written down for
Kaden Smith Kell

in dedication to anyone who has ever felt loss
of any kind.

In remembrance of

Trip

Jimmy

Watson

Emmalette

Darlett

Kollin

JR

Lynn

Kim

Tori

Jackson

Kaylla

Copyright © 2024

All Rights Reserved

ISBN:

978-1-964712-23-9 (Paperback)

978-1-964712-22-2(Hardcover)

978-1-964712-21-5 (Ebook)

Case id#: 1-14278521282

Table of Contents

Prologue

These are my memories of the events that made me question my reality, the following pages depicts the loss of my true loves. It chronicles my grief and pain that followed each loss.

It's about survival, and the appreciation I have for life.

And It's about letting go.

This memoir was intended to help others through tragedy. I had hoped it would be beneficial for myself as a form of therapy.

And this has been one of the best ideas I've ever had. With this experience I've been able to set it down, both figuratively and literally, letting it go.

By facing and embracing my reality I've found some closure. By reading this, you can carry some of the heaviness for me.

I've been running from my reality for too long and allowed the past to consume me. I've finally figured out how to stop running from and decided to run towards.

I've lived what feels like an infinite number of lifetimes in the time that it took to express my thoughts. Fuelled by my need to make something meaningful out of the senselessness, my creativity bleeding out, word by word.

Traveling the past paths as well as sharing them has filled me with both anxiety and relief, wave after wave of both. Expressing my perspective has been heavy and freeing simultaneously. I've repeated, this can't be reality as many times as it's expressed in the following pages. More actually...

It's raw.

It's tragic.

And, I hope it's inspiring.

This is the true story of my life.

This is my reality whether I want it to be or not.

And this memoir is my acceptance.

Introduction

My elevens hurt

I've referred to my elevens, the glabellar muscles on our forehead that wrinkle between our eyebrows, for years now in random conversations. Frowning and squinting are the common causes of muscle stimulation. Also a member of the worry line family, the muscles were nicknamed elevens, because they appear to be in pairs (11). I've used these muscles so much over my lifetime, I jokingly refer to any issue as messing with my elevens. And my elevens have been messed with a lot.

At some point during our lives we all experience situations that are impossible to accept. Life is simply complicated and trying to find the logic is often completely paradoxical. So we learn to question everything. We question people, their actions, words, and intentions. We question ourselves and our own perceptions, behaviors, and motivators. We question our purpose, and the need to understand can't always be satisfied.

This memoir chronicles the moments that made me question my reality. Acceptance is key, and it's taken me 45 years at this point to begin to process what life has thrown my way. I'm bitter, but better. And honestly my elevens always hurt....

Chapter 1

That Day

It's the 25th of Jan, the year 2018, and I'm heading home to feed our two furbabies lunch. This is normal for me as our kiddos eat three times a day and my job allowed the flexibility. However, my husband was working on his 18 wheeler at home that day, and was supposed to take care of the responsibility. I had been unable to contact him, but as he was working with his truck I didn't think twice before deciding to go home and feed them. His truck was his passion, and he found himself engrossed in projects frequently without realizing the time.

Pulling into our long gravel driveway I notice several vehicles parked in various places. It was 2:30 in the afternoon. Also not unusual as we had recently moved into our newly built home and contractors were in and out frequently. The guys were there working on our HVAC unit as scheduled. But as I noticed the other types of vehicles parked, sirens begin going off in my head. A woman I've never seen before begins walking towards my van, a pleasant but somber look on her face. She indicates for me to stay inside my vehicle.

Wait a minute, what?

"This is my house," I say to her. She responds with a friendly vibe, "No ma'am I need you to stay inside your vehicle, someone will be by to talk with you as soon as possible." My elevens are tight as the initial shock and confusion are outweighed by waves of fear and panic. I'm speechless for a moment, but don't move. I do as I'm told and stay seated inside the van.

Then the questions start flowing ... is my child ok, are my dogs ok, is anyone working in the house hurt ...? All of my questions are answered, "yes, as far as I know, the people you asked about are ok."

I sit there in disbelief thinking this can't be reality....

Chapter 2

A total Smith

Growing up living on a farm I had an epic childhood. I felt loved by my family, even though my parents expected a boy. My dad had two sisters, so being the only Smith made his desire for a son that much stronger. I was the hope to carry on our family name. When I arrived into this world a female that summer day in 1979, a favorite uncle offered a solution. He suggested my parents combine their first names. I hated it for the longest time but adore it now.

My sister and I were cared and provided for to the best of our parents abilities. They gifted us with the type of childhood you don't hear about anymore, before cell phones and the World Wide Web. Seriously we had three channels on our tv when I was a kid. If we were lucky they came in clear.

I lived down the street from my grandparents, and could quickly walk to their house which was beside our cow pasture. Raised Pentecostal Holiness, I was taught to say ma'am and sir, please and thank you.

Happy memories of my youth are filled with dirt roads and bicycles, snapping beans on grandma's porch, watering the most beautiful landscaping display with a bucket of Peter's Professional Plant Food, and playing in grandpa's old gas station shed. I had cats, bunnies, and even cows for pets. I made mud pies, climbed trees, and jumped on hay bales. I played in cotton fields and on cotton pickers. I had cousins and aunts and uncles and adored my family. I was a country girl. And a daddy's girl.

I was innocent, and it was amazing.

My Dad was my hero. The spitting image of Elvis, he had the lightest blue eyes I've ever seen. He was the high school football star and had a bright future ahead of him. He was a simple man, with simple goals although they were grand, and very handy with just about everything. I spent a lot of time with him just hanging out on the farm or in the shed while he tinkered away. Passionate and focused, he was well known and well liked throughout our community. His perspectives on life still shape many of mine. He wasn't perfect, but he was my daddy, and my sister and I both loved and respected him.

My mom was, well, my mother. And I adored her even though we didn't always agree. Her character can't be defined in just one word, but rather by a multitude of adjectives and nouns. She was simply an incredible woman that I learned many valuable lessons from. A majorette in high school, she could twirl a baton in ways that would blow your mind. She did well in school, and it's been said she had the best legs in her graduating class. She too was not perfect, but my sister and I loved her very much as well.

Our parents were both incredibly hard workers devoting long hours and dedication to their professions. Unfortunately their lives took them in separate directions, and they didn't agree on anything really. I remember being 10 yrs old when I realized my parents weren't happy together. My reality unraveled as I learned things I didn't understand. They should've divorced and found happiness elsewhere. But they thought being married was better for their daughters, even though the resentment between them worsened. As the years passed we grew accustomed to the negativity between them. My sister and I just accepted it as normal.

Being the baby of the family, my parents and older sister were a team when it came to raising me. As I've said, our parents worked long hours with their demanding occupations.

My father was a self-employed farmer, his hours consisted of all the time. All hours of the day when the sun provided light, he worked. When the sun went down he continued to work. He did sleep though. He was a great sleeper and I inherited that from him. Mom owned an Assisted Living Facility in town, 30 minutes away from the farm we lived on. The facility was open 24 hours a day, every day. So her hours were all the time as well. She could go for days without sleep. I still have no clue how she did that.

From the stories shared over the years, my sister was wonderful with me as a newborn. We bonded immediately even though there's a nine year age gap between us. Her birthday is coincidentally the day before mine so we grew up celebrating our special days together. She and I have been best friends since my birth, and still are to this day.

As I've said, my youth was epic. I broke both of my wrists, not concurrently, and earned a few scars during my farm life childhood. However, I did a complete 180 and at seven years old, I became a competitor in my first beauty pageant. From the ages of 7 to 15 I must've competed in over 200 pageants. The first one I had no clue how to even smile. Not a stage smile anyway. But I won Miss Congeniality and I was hooked. We really put effort into competitions. I took tap and jazz for talent and had an interview coach. I had custom made dresses and costumes. I wore rhinestone shoes that broke every time you wore them. I was a total girly girl.

It was my passion to compete and meet the other contestants, a total rush to be on stage. And I won many competitions, lost many too. During my pageant years some of the titles I represented are:

- Junior Miss Fiesta 1989
- Pre-Teen Ms South Carolina (Jr Miss) 1990
- Little Ms Chitlin Strut 1990 and again in 1996
- Young Ms Festival of Roses 1990 and again in 1994
- Young Miss Watermelon Festival 1991 and 1995
- Young Ms Ms Royal Beauty 1991
- Little Ms Egg Scramble Festival 1991
- Young Ms Railroad Daze 1992
- Young Ms Hell Hole Festival 1992

- Young Miss SC (LMSC) 1992
- Young Ms Angel of Beauty 1992
- Young Ms South Carolina's Most Beautiful 1992
- Junior Teen Miss Frog Jump 1994
- Teen Miss Peanut Festival 1994
- Queen of Queens National Young Miss 1994
- Junior Miss Wagons to Wagner 1995
- America's Calendar Miss February 1996
- Queen of Angels 1996
- Teen Miss Angel of the Universe 1997
- Miss South Congaree Western Weekend 1997
- Teen Miss Southern Bell 1997

I was even a Young Miss Tadpole at one point! I competed all over the state visiting different towns and festivals. I was in a rodeo and I even went on a cruise competing at the national level. I have a video of the evening I won my first state title in 1990. In the background you can hear my dad exclaiming, "that's my girl." Hearing him say that was one of the proudest moments of my youth.

I placed top 10 in the Teen Miss SC Pageant in 1994. The winner was someone we all thought highly of, and all the contestants had a blast during the preliminaries. She even won the national title of Teen Miss USA for our state that year. I never got the chance to tell her how proud I was and still am of her so if she's reading this, congratulations!!

The lifestyle was crazy and exciting and I had such a go, go, go, attitude. Little did I realize that would set the theme for my life. The valuable lessons provided made me realize I'm my own competitor. It's up to me to show up and represent, to be the best version of myself. And although I always tried to make the most out of every competition, sometimes I brought home a title, and sometimes I didn't. It was this opportunity that taught me everyone is special and unique. I am special and unique, but not always someone's choice. And that's ok.

My sister and I were a team, and I couldn't have done any of it without her. She is a leader and a supporter, and is unstoppable when she wants something. I looked up to her then as much as I do now. But since I'm nine years younger college took her away on a different adventure. She was my role model and influencer. And her departure from my every day life hit me hard.

The change was hard on her too, and she came home as often as she could, calling us nightly filling us in on the latest developments.

She is very determined, as I've pointed out. But she is also incredibly intelligent, possessing both book smarts and common sense. Before it seemed possible, she graduated with a nursing degree specializing in oncology and married her fiancé and boyfriend of over seven years. Frequently at my parents house working on mud trucks with my dad, he was part of the family and like a brother to me. He loved to call me little dude. I hated it at the time but the memory makes me smile.

Their wedding was like a fairytale, chandeliers in the tents, servers at the buffet, exquisite flowers and cake. The reception was indeed a party to remember. It was epic. It was magical. It was to me, the definition of love.

My dad had been diagnosed with renal cell cancer in 1993. He had complained of hip and joint pain for years before they finally discovered the source. He was stage II by the first diagnosis, and his prognosis looked grim with the expectancy rate less than three months without treatment. I was 14 at the time, and didn't understand all the medical terminology, but it's obvious they knew this was serious.

After surgery, chemotherapy, and radiation, he rang the bell and was cancer free.

My sister was actually his nurse during his stay on the oncology floor. And my mother was able to give many of his injections at home. His three years of treatments were absolutely miserable for him, but it was all worth it. My daddy had beat cancer and it was a miracle!!

1st Memoir

Chapter 3

It wasn't anyone's fault

Mom, Dad, and I are home the evening of June 18, 1996 when the phone rings. There's been an automobile accident. My sister's husband had been hurt and we needed to get to the scene immediately.

He was pronounced dead before we arrived.

Wait, what?

He just left our house. I just saw him. We should've been rushing to the hospital I realized later but no. There's no hope.

My sister didn't even know at this point. In a state of disbelief, mom, my cousin, and aunt loaded into our SUV and drove the hour to my sisters apartment. When we arrived and parked we could hear her screams echoing down from the 9th floor. She knew....

After some difficulty getting inside the secure building, we made our way up in the

13

elevator and hurried to her door. Her unit was at the very end of the hallway, and with each step her screams intensified.

I couldn't imagine the turmoil she was experiencing. What do you do in that situation? What do you say? How do you comfort someone in so much pain?

My 16 year old mind couldn't comprehend the magnitude of this loss. We will never see him again. We will never hear his laughter again. My sister was a widow at 25 yrs old. Married less than three months and still sending out thank you notes, her entire future altered unimaginably.

It wasn't her fault. It wasn't anyone's fault. So many mourned his death on so many different levels. Watching my sister's heart break over and over, again and again during the next weeks, I had no clue how she handled it.

She was so strong.

She wasn't given a choice.

Everything changed then. Life's fragility altered my perception of reality. There were typical highs and lows of teenage life. Some not as typical as my peers but normal'ish. I argued with my parents and rebelled a bit. Sounds normal to me....

That very same summer of '96, before my senior year of high school, my family received yet another call. I had been involved in an automobile accident. My friend was driving us when a car T-boned the driver's side of her vehicle. She was badly injured and thrown on top of me when the impact happened. I don't remember any of the accident even though witnesses attest to my screams for hours. It's as if I blinked before we were hit and opened my eyes on the stretcher in the ambulance, a lovely woman's face above me, asking if she could cut my belt and pants off. I remember asking her why she would need to do that and she informed me gently that I had been in a vehicle accident.

Wait, what?

Then I felt the pain. Or I realized I was in pain. I'm not sure how to explain it. I remember repeating my leg!! my leg!! over and over and over and over. My friends told me later they could hear me screaming from the waiting room.

It flipping hurt. Scans and x-rays revealed my left femur (thigh bone) was shattered near the top and fractured in the middle. I would need a titanium rod to stabilize the break. An operation later and I'm bionic woman, without the super powers.

This was a hard time for my family and for myself. The physicians quickly realized I'm majorly allergic to opioids. So I was sick on top of injured. I couldn't eat, was nauseated all the time, and developed a rash from the meds. So codeine was out, enters ibuprofen. Ibuprofen didn't touch the pain I felt but there aren't many alternatives. Physical therapy was brutal, my therapist was amazing, but the car crash and surgery tore muscles and tendons. Everything had to be repaired and strengthened. Learning to lift my leg and walk again included many tears and complaints. And I was dependent on help for everything. I couldn't shower, go to the bathroom, even get out of bed by myself for what seemed like an eternity. At 16 yrs old I lost all the independence I had matured into. I was a child all over again.

My friend who was driving fared much worse though, suffering broken ribs, pelvis, a collapsed lung, spinal injuries, and the list goes on. She still has major pain to this day. She's a strong woman though and I've witnessed her overcome many obstacles! So if she's reading this, you've got this, always!

The farm I lived on was 30 minutes away from school. So that meant I couldn't easily catch a ride with friends to and from home. I loved my Mother but she was consistently late. Arriving with my mom after the tardy bell as a senior on crutches ...let's just say I wasn't the cheeriest person to be around. A very sweet friend would sometimes leave his home an hour before school to come and pick me up. The memories of those mornings jamming out and gossiping about things that didn't matter are priceless to me and I really appreciated his friendship. Still do.

My senior year of high school I entered the gymnasium for the first day pep rally on crutches with a rod running the length of my left femur held in place by two very large screws. By my senior class trip to DC, I was walking without crutches. But I was miserable, trying to keep up with the group. An AP Honors class trip to Spain was grueling, so much walking. Both were amazing and unforgettable trips of a lifetime, but traversing those winding streets and enormous monuments and cathedrals were challenging.

Simply put, it was painful. I physically hurt for many years following the car wreck and every now and then the shattered area aches. The only thing I can be grateful for is that I haven't grown since the accident. If I had hit a growth spurt obviously my rod would not have grown with me and I would've walked with a limp. At 45 I think I'm safe from growing any more. Shrinking maybe, but not growing.

Chapter 4

The Dogwoods

It was then that I started my college era. I was loving life and managing all my obligations. Honored to be accepted into the college of my choice. I moved into my sister's old unit on the 9th floor while she occupied a unit on the top floor. I was excelling in school in the pre-pharmacy program and received a certificate from the National Academic Honor Society for Freshman. My family and I were all so proud!!

As far as relationships are concerned, I had a few. My first boyfriend and I dated for a year when I was 13 and he was 15. We were serious pretty fast and he was a great guy. Like a really decent human being. But we were young, and it didn't last. I dated a few other guys during high school, some more serious than others. My first real relationship with any depth didn't happen until college. That's when I met a really cool guy. Like really cool, and I was into him before he started pursuing me. We dated for 3 years, mostly very happy years. But we were young and again, it didn't last.

I had several somewhat serious relationships during my 20's, some of them really great. I had my heart broken a few times, and other times I was responsible for breaking their hearts. Looking back at my 26 yr old self with my 45 year old perspective, I now recognize and appreciate the lessons I learned, no matter how the relationships ended.

I made some amazing friends, truly genuine people, and have so many fun, scary and crazy memories with them. We have a group, lovingly named The Dogwoods due to a very special woman and the necklace she was wearing one evening. It was obviously a dogwood pendant with its signature four delicate petals and we were a group of four. It was silly and cute and cheesy, but it stuck.

Our crew consisted of more than just us four though. And those who are Dogwoods know they are Dogwoods. We all have been through so much together, and we're all different, yet the same. Our favorite thing to do honestly was just hang out together. Going to clubs and parties seemed pointless when we could just hang at the OG Dogwood's house.

However we did enough clubbing in our day, so no worries there.

Actually my favorite place was and still is a cozy bar and the bartender, whom I adore, is now there as the owner. My Dogwoods and I went and still go sit at the round table whenever the opportunity presents itself. That table has hosted us for birthdays and celebrations of life milestones alike, not to mention the time spent there two decades ago. If that table could speak it would have so many stories it could tell.

I was so beyond blessed with their friendships and still am to this day. We were always together, and unlike some college friendships ours have stood the test of time. We still assemble for various events, birthdays, holidays, sleepovers and vacations, even after all this time.

And my family increased by three!! My sister found love again with a man my son affectionately calls iron man. Being a pilot, he literally swept her off her feet. After getting to know each other more, he proposed and I had a brother-in-law and step nephew! Their wedding was also an event to remember, my favorite memory including my sister, her new husband, his son, and my father sitting on the seat of one of his John Deere tractors. A few years later they added another son to their family. This is not my story to tell, but they are still happily living the go, go, go lifestyle and my nephews have both grown up to be remarkable young men.

Chapter 5

Knight in shining Ford

The Dogwoods and I formed this bond before the pressure of life got to me. I went through a crisis phase, feelings of inadequacy and fears of failure controlling my thoughts. And the self induced stress was unbearable. It was at this stage of my life that I made many bad decisions. Like a lot of them.

Looking back it was the only thing I really got correct. I dropped out of the six-year Doctorate of Pharmacy program I had worked so hard to get into and transferred my credits to receive an Associate's Degree in Science. I had excelled for years getting A's in organic chemistry and physics, and I learned so many valuable things along the way. But coming from a six-year program ending up with an Associate's Degree, I was so lost when my husband trucked into my life.

I was 27 when my husband and I first officially met. I will always treasure the way our paths crossed. We had known of each other for years but hadn't actually had a conversation until the day he rescued me.

Like with my sister, my future husband adored my father, and they worked on his passion together, mud trucks. Spending hours in the mud racing shiny expensive trucks is an epic experience. My dad's truck, The Color of Money, won many events, but not all of them. The lessons learned here reinforced my principles picked up from my pageant era. The theme of making the best out of any situation, win or lose, is the takeaway. Show up, have the best attitude you can manage, put your effort into what you value, and have pride in every accomplishment. The prize isn't the trophy anyway, the experience is.

I'm out of town one afternoon and my Honda's transmission decided to act crazy. Of course I called my dad for help. My father, who was on a tractor in the field at the time, actually sent my husband to rescue me. From that point on I nicknamed him my Knight in shining Ford! His truck was lifted so high he had to pick me up to get me into it. The Ford was custom, immaculate, and larger than life, just like he was. And I was head over heels smitten with the man behind the wheel. Our connection, instant and powerful, was felt by us both.

My husband was only 19 years old when his mother passed away. His parents were divorced and his mother remarried when he was young. His childhood was not the most affectionate, and I'm grateful his grandmother and step-father's family played such a huge role in his life. I credit them for his sweet disposition.

He was a good man - simple, honest, dependable, funny, genuine, a man's man, the kind of man who would literally give you the shirt off his back. He was a true gentleman, and had a heart of pure gold. He was the guy who bought burgers for random dogs on his travels. He was the friend that would call and chat for hours about anything. He never talked bad or down to anyone. He didn't compete with others, only himself. And he wanted everyone to be happy. He believed wholeheartedly that we all have the right and freedom to choose our own happiness. This belief is one of many he and I shared.

He was the alpha to my beta. He was the leader and I was our cheerleader. Excited by everything, he saw so much potential in everyone where others didn't. And it was contagious. He taught me how to love and be loved. He made me a believer, saving me in so many ways besides just my Honda....

My husband proposed to me on my 29th birthday with the most exquisite engagement ring I've even seen, a white gold 1.2 carat princess cut diamond solitaire set diagonally surrounded by a halo of round diamonds, with more round diamonds trailing each shank. On each side of the donut, the bottom base that sits on the flank housing the stones, rests a yellow gold heart. Saying yes to him is another beautiful memory I will always treasure.

Originally we would spend time together at my 9th floor apartment or his home. I was my husband's second wife, and he had shared his home with his ex and then later with his roommate. This roommate, who is also a friend, still checks on us to this day. As our relationship deepened, we moved into a condo together. We spent a lovely year there, but the condo was a greater distance from our jobs than desired. So we called a realtor and embarked on a journey of house hunting, choosing to put down roots in the town I grew up in.

Naturally there's a lot to consider when picking your ideal property. Mortgages, credit scores, and down payments can be intensely overwhelming. After analyzing and studying our options, we made an offer on a home we fell in love with! Our realtor called us with the disappointing update that our offer was rejected. The house was active contingent, meaning they had accepted a previous offer.

We continued our search, although feeling defeated, and came across a home in a lovely subdivision. Not wasting a moment our agent submitted our offer, and after a bidding war, we were officially first time home owners! We added an adorable feisty little puppy to our family, and continued building our life.

Our first furbaby was spoiled rotten by us both. My husband was great with her, training her to sit and stay and shake. She was obsessed with yellow squeaky balls and could catch them in the air with her teeth. She drove us absolutely bonkers when one rolled under the couch. She would whine and wag her tail indicating what she wanted until one of us got up to fetch her ball. We purchased new couches without raised legs on them soon after she entered our lives.

We were in the process of buying our first house when my Dad passed away. After a 15 yr remission, his cancer had returned and spread.

His first fight against the disease had been almost impossible to endure the first time, and had returned with a vengeance.

He underwent more treatments and we were all hopeful he would beat it again. He was such a strong man, we had so much confidence that it was possible. But it wasn't meant to be. A year of agonizing drug cocktails and chemotherapy, and my father was informed the last protocol available was no longer effective.

As we sat in his oncologist's office, I heard and saw and felt our hope being taken away from us. I didn't look at my father, we just sat there staring at the oncologist, waiting for more. More suggestions, more answers, more reasons to fight, we waited for more of anything but none came. My daddy's cancer was growing and there were no more options to try. His physician gave him six months to live.

The unexpected news came as a shock to us all. That same June evening in 2009 he called his loved ones to come and visit, telling them the results of the scan and telling them what we later realized was goodbye. He left this world less than 48 hours later.

The day of his funeral my family walked to the church from our family home, down the street from my grandparents' house. My soon to be husband holding my hand, I found the strength to put each foot in front of the other. My father, my hero, passed away before his 65th birthday. Blessed with him as my father for 29 years, he was an inspiration of a man, and my son has many of his characteristics.

Almost a year later my fiancé became my husband! We were wedded in an absolutely gorgeous ceremony and I have amazing memories that I will cherish always. From the lavish pergola setting adorned with breathtaking flower arrangements, the personalized M&M's on the candy table display with our faces on them, to my dream wedding dress and the incredible cake that matched my dress, it was almost exactly how I envisioned. (It was much hotter that May than I had anticipated) Pink and John Deere green were our colors, and our furbaby was the flower girl pulled on a pink radio flyer wagon by my adorable nephew. A Dogwood even sang beautifully at our ceremony. Our vows were emotional as our pastor joined us in till death do us part. My sister gave a amazing toast at the reception, and we were celebrated leaving our wedding in that beautiful Ford truck, that again, I was lifted into....

My husband reveled at the ceremony, talking with everyone and he was so at ease and handsome. He was happy, and I fell in love with him even more that day.

Since my Dad couldn't be there to walk me down the aisle, I'm forever grateful my uncle stepped in and gave me away. There's even a photo of us featured in the 2010 Summer/Fall issue of Carolina Bride Magazine, page 52. But it's natural for a bride to want her father on her wedding day. I placed an orchid on his empty chair beside my mother as my tears fell next to it. His absence was felt by all, but by my husband and myself the most.

Our honeymoon consisted of a Disney trip with our new puppy. My husband refused to fly and hated riding in anything he wasn't in control of. So I was a passenger princess and yes, our furbaby went with us. She went riding with her daddy in his 18 wheeler as well. She got so much attention!! We couldn't leave her behind, ever, and it was a known fact that our furbaby went wherever we did.

<u>Chapter 6</u>

Building our future

My husband started driving tractor trailers when he was 18 years old. He was good at it. And everyone knew it. My favorite thing to do was ride with him on my days off. I remember having to get in the back going through the mountains in Tennessee, the drop-offs being infinitely more intimidating in a rig versus a car.

His business was booming and he was always busy getting new contracts. He drove a purple Kenworth at that time, and it was his baby, his pride and joy. Custom everything, he had decked it out in chrome with diamond plated panels and extensive interior and exterior lighting. He put this much effort into everything he did.

When we married he stopped traveling long distance so he could be home at night. The pay wasn't as much as when he hauled Over The Road, but he took a gamble on himself as an owner-operator with the desire to be near his family. It was a very good bet. He expanded his business, adding equipment that allowed him to haul any substance. He invested his grandmother's inheritance on a black Peterbuilt, of course with custom purple and chrome accents and diamond plated panels. And with this growth he accomplished his dream of forming his trucking company in 2013. We were beyond happy and proud of his accomplishments.

As for my occupation, my grandmother started one of the first Community Assisted Living Care Facilities in the state. My mom was her administrator until she took over in 1980. I followed in her footsteps as the new administrator in 2008, and later the owner in 2013. With my background in pharmacy and being a part of the facility growing up, it seemed a natural fit.

Since the facility had been in the family my entire lifetime, I spent my youth around people who needed care. This usually meant elderly or those in need of rehabilitation.

And I loved it.

I learned so much from their wisdom, and had so much attention as a child! However the facility was vastly different from an adult's perspective. It's challenging, and requires a strength that most don't possess. I rarely witnessed residents improve or return home. I did appreciate my job and gained so many valuable lessons surrounded by incredible men and women, both residents and staff. But it's a vibe and the role of caregiver is all encompassing.

We weren't in a hurry to have children, but knew we wanted to build a life and family together. When the time came to put effort into getting pregnant, the excitement and anticipation felt by us both was an amazing high. We were in love with each other and in love with the idea of growing as a family.

We discussed increasing our household by another half, as we wanted another furbaby, to love and to have a friend for our first little angel. So we added a second puppy into our home and hearts. She was full of rich colors, auburn, chocolate, and caramel, but after her first trim her hair lost all of its pigmentation. My husband said she must've been an angel since God turned her white. With our two furbabies playing together and bonding as sisters, the cuteness overload brought so much joy to us both!!

A year goes by, and at my yearly physical I'm prescribed Clomid, the first of many hormones I would take to increase our odds of getting pregnant. Months go by with negative after negative pregnancy tests, so our Dr. suggested a specific lab performed. The process was a tricky one to do but we managed it. Twice actually because the first results were flawed. Or so we thought. The second sample gave the same conclusion as the first. A secretary from our physicians office called me with the lab results. While I was driving, I was informed that my husband and I would not be able to have children.

My phone in my hand, behind the steering wheel of a moving vehicle my lungs forgot to expand and compress.

Wait a minute, what..?

This can't be reality....

Chapter 7

IVF is not romantic

After safely returning to the assisted living facility and falling apart, I called our OBGYN's office back to speak with the actual physician as the secretary didn't know anything about, well, anything, at all. I'm fuming and panicked, crying and confused as to what these results actually meant for our family.

When I finally speak with our physician, it's reiterated that we would need to see a specialist if we had any hopes of achieving pregnancy. She explained some technical details that at the time I didn't understand. But there was hope provided in our conversation, and it fueled the mission to seek assistance. After discussing financial, moral, and religious dilemmas many, many times, my husband and I both agreed to seek answers and help.

Fertility clinic here we come!

IVF or In Vitro Fertilization is a world of its own. It's a fertility treatment combining individual eggs and sperm in a lab to create embryos. There are many variations and options to choose from depending on each couple's needs.

Our protocol manipulated my reproductive cycle to release multiple eggs which were surgically retrieved and prepared for fertilization. ICSI (intracytoplasmic sperm injection) was then carefully performed on each egg retrieved in the hopes of becoming an embryo. The process continues in the following steps.

- If each sperm and egg merge, fertilization has occurred. The conditions have to be ideal in order for that single cell to then split, dividing and multiplying into more cells. Three days after fertilization, if the zygote's cells continued to increase and expand, transfer into the uterus occurs. Around five days after fertilization, the implanted zygote develops into an blastocyst next, and then into an embryo.
- 7 to 10 days later the placenta begins to form and releases enough hCG (human chorionic gonadotropin) to be

detectable on a pregnancy test. If all of these factors miraculously line up perfectly and positive results are achieved, more labs, tests and medications follow. The fertility specialists continue monitoring the mommy and embryo(s) until 7 to 10 weeks of pregnancy. At that point they release you to your Obstetrician's care.

IVF is a perilous journey into the unknown. Every aspect is intimidating. And there are no guarantees. All of the steps I mentioned must occur in perfect harmony in order to achieve a viable pregnancy. There are nurses and doctors and blood draws. There are scans and probes and surgeries. There are oral and injectable medications and the stress of getting it all correct is an issue in itself.

And the hormones - God bless my husband for dealing with my hormones. Extreme moods swings resulted from the multiple drug regimens. My temperament all over the place at times, from one extreme to the other. It's the least romantic experience I can imagine when the goal is procreation.

And I absolutely hate needles. A widely suggested adjunct for improving pregnancy rates is acupuncture. I was already doing everything in the book, even burning fertility incense... so sign me up, whatever it takes.

Acupuncture is all based upon using tiny hair like needles to stimulate pressure points and increase blood flow. I did not enjoy this therapy, even though my acupuncturist was amazing. I must've been in his office over 100 times during the course of my IVF journey. In addition, the hormones I mentioned consisted of both oral and injectable medications. I was expected and required to self inject these hormones sometimes three times a day, several injections per time period.

I almost passed out the first time I stuck a needle into my own stomach. It's the second time in my life I can remember seeing stars floating around in my vision while losing my balance. The first when I got my belly button pierced - again, I hate needles. It took over an hour of trying and panicking while my mother encouraged and supported me. She caught me in her arms the moment I started to fall out of the chair when the stars appeared. After the first needle was self-injected, each one was a little easier. And yet each one was as hard as the first.

The intramuscular progesterone injections were the worst though. That's a very big needle and the shots left huge bruise marks. And they are commonly prescribed in fertility treatments, twice a day for sometimes months. To all those who have, are, or will travel this journey, I applaud you. It's not easy but it's worth it when it works.

And it was worth it to me even when it didn't. There are many people who helped to give my injections when I couldn't, and for them I'm eternally grateful. Eventually my dear husband gave all the IM injections. He became very good at it and for that I was equally impressed and appreciative, and my bruising eventually improved. I can't tell you enough how amazing a man he really was.

Our first attempt at IVF was crazy and confusing and, what I was convinced, would be a total disaster.

But it was a success.

Wait, what?

When I woke up from the anesthesia I was sick as usual, I just don't do well with strong medications. But it didn't matter, we had three zygotes form after ICSI was performed. We couldn't believe this news. As the days progressed the third one did not make it to embryo stage.

On September 23rd, 2012, my husband and I arrived for the procedure to transfer the two embryos into my uterus. We went home and waited the suggested 7-10 days to test. Well, I tried to wait anyway. On day 3, 4, and 5 the tests were negative. But on day 6, I had two very, very, faint lines appear! Actually they didn't show up immediately after the specified time on the instructions. It was an hour after I took the first test on that 6th day that I noticed the faint lines. Of course I re-tested and almost fell to the floor. I couldn't believe the process had resulted in back to back positive pregnancy tests. I say back to back because I kept taking the tests, I needed verification. To be honest I tested every day for the first month, just to ease my anxiety.

Continuing needles and tests and acupuncture, and we finally saw our miracle baby's heartbeat, a flicker on the ultrasound monitor. It was one the most beautiful sights I've ever seen. And one of the best feelings of my life. To say we were elated is an understatement!

Creation is truly a miracle. Knowing the process more detailed than the average person

I am shocked so many babies are born. As I've said, It's not easy to attain pregnancy and not all result in live births.

My husband and I attended a football game during our pregnancy in 2012, with my fellow Dogwoods. One of my friends happened to be pregnant at the same time! We were too early to announce it so we pretended to drink alcohol. It was the first game either of us had been to completely sober. Let's just say it's a different experience! But we had fun pretend drinking all the same, and I have really great memories from that event.

Not long after the game, my fellow pregnant Dogwood called me with test results involving her baby boy. She did not have a viable pregnancy and would lose the baby. Our hearts broken, none more than hers and her husbands, we struggled to find the answers, to understand the why. This again is not my story to tell. But I will say she and her husband now have a gorgeous, smart, witty, loving daughter a few months younger than my son! And the most amazing part, our kids have grown up to be best friends, affectionately named the Little Dogwoods.

To say we were worried my entire pregnancy would be putting it lightly.

Miscarriages are common in my family and my anxiety was through the roof. We couldn't lose our baby.

Before our son's arrival my husband's beloved grandmother passed away. Losing her was abrupt and left us all deeply saddened. She had filled the role of mother for my husband and I'm grateful she saw ultrasound photos of her great grandson. She was an incredible woman and I absolutely adored her. My husband and I mourned her absence in our lives, and grieved the fact our son would never have the chance to meet her.

As my husband's father was disabled, with her passing he no longer had care. As a growing family, we decided he needed assistance beyond what we were able to personally provide. He therefore moved into my assisted living facility, where he remains to this day.

My husband's father, affectionately called Papa by our son, would visit us every Sunday in our first home, a pattern that we adored. He was very involved with our second home too. His presence meant so much to our family.

Chapter 8

Boys will be boys

Our worries throughout the pregnancy were unfounded, thankfully! Our miracle baby boy arrived on June 5th, the anniversary of my dad's passing, to bring his light into our world. I was 33 years old, my husband 35.

He was born healthy with my mom, sister, aunt, cousin, and my husband all present in the hospital room. Delivery wasn't easy but after the epidural I was fine. No horror stories to tell, and the experience was actually amazing and miraculous.

Mommy and Daddy did great as newborn parents! Our son's progress in the hospital following his birth was reassuring, going exceptionally well. Breast feeding was tricky but once we got the latching technique we were rocking it! He was such an amazing newborn, right up until we left the delivery floor.

I swear the moment after being released to go home, our son started crying. With all three of us in tears, we tried everything! And I mean everything we could think of, and everything suggested to us, but were unable to ease his discomfort. Our sweet baby wailed for hours until we returned to the ER, both my husband and I overcome with fear and concern.

Thankfully they discovered he wasn't receiving enough milk and was dehydrated. We had no way of knowing he needed supplemental milk as we we're doing great in the hospital. But as his needs increased, my milk supply couldn't keep up. I was crushed but my husband kept on trucking. We purchased a breast pump and I mixed my supply with formula. Once our sweet newborn had relief and a full belly, we were rocking as parents again!!

To everyone who has in any way experienced breast feeding struggles, my heart goes out to you.

Besides the usual mishaps our son was perfect and so was our life. From his kicking while pregnant my husband and I predicted he would be left handed. As he matured from the newborn phases he proved our intuitions correct. He did the boot scoot crawl before walking, and took the normal tumbles when learning to stand upright. He even suffered a broken collarbone when he was one and a half years old, but that's a story in itself.

He was curious and creative and a miracle to behold. He was always a great sleeper, just like me, and was a great baby in general. His presence filled our home with so much meaning. He had the most contagious baby laugh I've ever heard. His laughter is still contagious.

This is the best time of that life. Happiness radiated out of us, the proud parents, as we tried our best to figure out parenting.

There's no manual and each child is different. We were a team but my husband was so amazing as a father! I still to this day have never met a man so gentle and absolutely smitten with his child. He wanted to hold him constantly. He played with him. He giggled and chatted with him. He laughed with him and made us laugh. I was in Heaven. Our family, including the furbabies, couldn't be touched. Everything was beyond perfect....

Our son was and is still the coolest person I've ever met. And my husband felt the same way. He was so involved with him, all of us attending soccer practice and games, karate classes and basketball. My husband went over the top for his son. He customized an electric 4-wheeler with vinyl stickers of the Transformers emblem, in red and blue just like Optimus Prime. He had a custom kid size electric tractor trailer that had an unreasonably loud horn. We even had a camper we had intended to take to racing events. Like my father, my husband enjoyed racing dirt bikes, 4-wheelers, and of course, mud trucks.

We had plans, big ones, and they included quality time as a family. And for a man that hated to be in pictures, he sure snapped tons of his son and wife. He was proud of us and it showed!

Two of the most fantastic years pass. My husband and I were doing well in our occupations and our son was growing up to be a delightful little boy. He had us both wrapped around his little fingers. We decided the time had come to try again as we wanted another child to love, and we wanted our children to each have a sibling.

Fertility clinic here we come...again!

Attempt #2 didn't go well.

Nothing.

Absolutely nothing.

I mean absolutely nothing.

Wait, what...?

This can't be reality is the only thought I had when I woke up from the anesthesia. It's not common to get absolutely zero. The cycle was over for me right then and there. No hope to take home and no need for the stack pile of pregnancy tests I had collected. I was completely crushed and confused, but survived my first failed IVF protocol with the help of another Dogwood, coincidentally undergoing the same fertility cycle. Her outcome was much better than mine, as she was pregnant with twins! My happiness for her superseded my own disappointment, thankfully. Her life is beautifully complex and fascinating and again, it's her story to tell. But she is thriving and has found happiness and sees blessings through the hardships.

Fast-forward through IVF attempts three to six. To summarize, my husband was busy being amazing, our son getting cooler by the second, and I was in obsessive mode. Some of the attempts led to transfers with healthy embryos. However, the two pink lines were impossible to attain. Every negative test broke another piece of my heart. For me, everything revolved around IVF. I was focused primarily on my health, consuming every vitamin and suggested treatment for infertility and avoiding xenoestrogens at all inconvenience. That's not a printing error, I meant inconvenience because everything I did or didn't do centered on the hope that I had control over something.

And the control primarily included eliminating as much plastic in my routine as possible. I had control over the water I drank, filtered only out of a glass. We didn't use plastic containers and I avoided caffeine, even gave up coffee all together. I made vitamin shakes and ingested so many supplements daily. Honestly it was exhausting and on top of all the prescribed hormone therapies and repeated failed cycles, I was not the most pleasant to be around.

I even became gluten free by choice to increase our chances. I do not have Celiac disease, and back then gluten free was hard to find. I remember being at Disney with my husband, our then three year old son, my sister and nephew, and waiting for two hours because my food and bread had to be specially made. We missed our fast pass rides and everyone was unhappy because of my obsession, including myself.

After each failed attempt we would both agree, no more IVF. Then a few months would go by and the obsession would rage uncontrollably. My husband thought we were being greedy and should stop. That it wasn't meant to be.

But I managed to convince him to go another round every time. I pleaded this can't be reality, over and over. He loved me, but most importantly he had so much love to share that only magnified with our son's arrival. So he caved and let me have my way. Always....

The IVF lows are no joke. They can break you. They can tear your heart to shreds, they can destroy relationships, marriages, bank accounts. It's a hard road to tread.

But we survived it.

And it made us stronger.

1st Memoir

Chapter 9

A wedding and a funeral

April 28th, 2017 was a day The Dogwoods were anticipating! Honored to be part of the wedding party celebrating my bestie's nuptials, the day went by so incredibly fast. It was a beautiful Catholic wedding, including tons of sitting and standing. My family looked amazing decked out in purple, my husband's favorite color. The reception was gorgeous, beaming faces, twinkling lights, it was like a dream. The memories are definitely surreal....

One of the Dogwoods was not at the ceremony. While the wedding procession walked out of the beautiful catholic church to eager guests, our friends grabbed me and whispered the news of her whereabouts. As I had been with the bride all day, our friends explained our missing Dogwood had been taken to the hospital after suffering a brain aneurysm earlier that day.

Wait, what?

I continued walking with the wedding procession in a state of absolute shock and confusion. We took photos and made our way to the reception, the entire time my thoughts centered on our friend. It wasn't until the reception had progressed some that I found any clarity. The only clarity they had to give. While getting ready for our friends long awaited and celebrated nuptials, she had complained of a headache and passed out. They called EMS and as they weren't allowed to accompany her, continued to proceed to the church.

How do you really define an aneurysm?

Is an aneurysm an accident? A twist of fate? How do you explain that? What are the odds? Where was the lesson? How were we supposed to make sense of this?

The unexpected tragedy shook us all to the core. We had high hopes she would recover. The initial reports looked encouraging giving us confidence her health would improve. Her attending physicians faced many challenges but kept coming up with solutions. However, as the updates continued over the next few days, her condition worsened. She left us on May 3rd, 2017.

This can't be reality.

She was a woman I admired and looked up to. She was a proud mother of her two amazing children, (grown-ups now - and still amazing!) and beamed as a grandmother. She adored her grandson and was over the moon excited about her granddaughter's upcoming birth.

She was a talented artist with eyes that saw with such beauty she radiated it herself. Her personality and energy were in a word, mesmerizing. If anyone can be described as having flair, it's her, and her art and style reflected this. She was complicated but simple. She was tough and she was gentle. She was a survivor who had made difficult decisions in her life.

I admired her strength of conviction and self awareness more than anyone I've ever met. To this day when I think about her, it's equivalent to personal life goals. Simply put she was the OG. She brought us all together. I loved her very much, all of us did, and losing her was devastating. It wasn't something any of us could understand so I did what I do. I mourned to the point of breaking then ran from it. Kept my mind focused on my mission - my goal was my family.

1st Memoir

Chapter 10

The flicker

On our 7th In Vitro attempt I didn't even test early. If you know, you know. The cycle had been typical but resulted in successful fertilization and embryo development. On May 30th, 2017 we were scheduled for surgery, and we even had embryos left over to freeze, five total strong healthy boys! We made the decision to have one embryo delicately transferred in hopes of implantation. We then went home to pray and wait. You cannot imagine my lack of belief when those two red lines appeared on that first pregnancy test.

Hallelujah we were pregnant!

I repeated the test five times to be exact, before calling my husband to share the news. We were both shocked and elated simultaneously!

The sight of our baby's heartbeat flicker on the ultrasound monitor was the second most beautiful sight to us both! We were going to have another baby boy, and my world was full of rainbows and butterflies and sunshine. As time went on and my pregnancy progressed, we felt comfortable revealing our news with the world and with our son. We announced our Valentine's due date and to say everyone was excited would be putting it lightly. Heck it was a flipping miracle!

All three of us, especially our son, were overjoyed. My husband and I picked out and read books filled with stories of brothers and siblings. We discussed many details about sharing, and being a good role model by setting a good example. Our son was so excited to become a big brother!

And we were busy building our dream home on our dream property. My husband wanted land. As an Owner/Operator of an 18-wheeler, he needed space for his equipment and room to store his tankers and trailers. Although we loved the neighborhood we lived in, and especially our neighbors, we decided to put the house our family started out in up for sale. After putting time and effort into renovating the home, removing walls, gutting the master bathroom , even adding an in-ground pool, it was a difficult decision to make. However we called our realtor and began making plans. Leaving behind the streets I walked my two furbabies on every day, we chose to embark on our dream adventure together.

We picked out a quiet ten acre lot close to town and next to our son's school. We found our house plans and contractor, and planned our happily ever after. My husband took so much pride in everything he did, and the house was no exception. Watching my husband see our shared dream come to fruition, I fell in love with him more and more each day. We both enjoyed the process of creating our dream home more than what you would expect. But he was beyond happy, helping hammer in nails and assisting whenever he could. He wanted to be a part of it. That's just the kind of man he was.

Of course there were challenges, but we really came together as a family, even adding another furbaby, our rescue, to the crew. He was saved from a house next door to my facility, with the intent of becoming a therapy dog for the residents. I brought him home with me until he could get properly vaccinated. But this mischievous silly little guy worked his way into all our hearts and became our newest family member! My first male dog and first rescue dog, he kept me busy and entertained for sure. I've learned the hard way not to underestimate him.

So there I was, a wife to an incredible man, a mom of a super cool four year old, 19 weeks pregnant and glowing, and the time came for us to move into our new residence. Life was flipping great. Like I smiled all the time. I had everything I ever wanted and so much more. We were on top of the world.

Chapter 11

Tiny hands and tiny feet

September 26, 2017 was a typical afternoon. I was driving back to work from an errand a few minutes before four o'clock, when a county van backed out of their driveway not seeing me approaching. I tried to avoid hitting them but was unable to do so. I slammed on the brakes, my seatbelt tightened, and my head hit the steering wheel. When I sat back up following the impact, white powder from the air bag filled the air, and I was in immediate shock. My first thought was of course our baby. I jumped out of the van instinctively assessing myself. I tried to stay calm until EMS arrived and checked our unborn son's pulse. His little heart was beating strong!

Panicked I had called my husband immediately and he rushed to the scene, picking up our son from daycare on the way. Concerned about our baby and I, they took me to pick up a rental car and then we headed to the hospital emergency room for a full check up as suggested. The waiting room was packed and I really didn't want my family sitting there any longer than necessary. So at my insistence, my husband and son went home while I remained in the lobby waiting. My sister begged me to let her come sit with me, but I was not having it. I'm fine, everyone is busy and there's no need to lose sleep and drive in the middle of the night, I told her.

Eventually I was called back to the emergency department to get checked out. It was around ten o'clock in the evening . Again they checked mine and the baby's stats, and all looked normal, strong even. I couldn't be transferred up due to hospital lockdown policies and made it to the OB floor around 12:15 in the morning of Sept 27, 2017.

The nurses needed to check all stats and vitals yet again for a baseline before I could rest. I remember being completely exhausted and super uncomfortable. Everything they checked with me looked fine, again, normal. However, the baby's heartbeat proved to be impossible to find with the stethoscope. The nurse said the ultrasound machine would find his heartbeat for sure and the on call specialist would bring it in asap.

She left the room and my breathing became difficult. As I waited on the Doctor to arrive I tried to stop the intrusive thoughts I was being bombarded with. Something isn't right I thought, but I was confident our baby was ok. Doubt kept creeping in but I pushed it aside. Logic and hope fighting each other in a dramatic show of despair raged in my mind. I knew our boy was strong and my pregnancy viable. Everything would be ok.

After what seemed like an eternity the specialist came in and spoke with me while plugging the ultrasound machine up. The monitor came to life and as it powered on my anxiety eased for just a moment. The familiarity of the machine reminding me of the fertility clinic, my faith and confidence surged. But as he pushed the wand around my swollen belly looking for our son's pulse, my breath got stuck in my airway. My lungs forgot to expand and contract again.

There was no flicker.

There was no heart beat.

Wait, what just happened....

Our son was pronounced dead at 20 weeks gestational age. During the accident my seatbelt damaged his umbilical cord and there was nothing they could've done. There was nothing they could do. There was no hope to give. At 20 weeks I had begun to feel his little kicks, he had a name, he had a nursery waiting on him in the new house....

This can't be reality....

What do I do, I'm in the hospital alone and everyone is asleep and I don't want to wake them up and don't call anyone, I don't want them to know.

I don't want this to be real.

I broke into pieces, the initial confusion and shock replaced by intense grief. Eventually I attempted calling my sister but my phone was dead. I called from other numbers but she didn't answer them. It's 1:45 in the morning, why would she...? After what feels like days the nurses found a way to charge my phone, and I made the dreaded call to tell her our baby didn't survive the accident. Of course she rushed to the hospital, picking up my aunt and cousin on the way. The intent was to bring my husband to the hospital with them, and our son would stay at our house with my aunt.

Wait, no, you're not disrupting my family. Do not call my husband. I cried to her, do not tell him, don't tell my son.

It can't be I told her.

No.

This was the version of myself that couldn't handle it and couldn't face the truth. I had perfected my skills of denial after everything we had been through. It was over, there was nothing to hope for, and I just wanted, needed to block it out. Once everyone knew I could no longer pretend this wasn't my reality. I begged her to leave me in my little secluded hospital room all alone. This pattern I picked up as a form of survival. Too many unexplainable experiences taught me to compartmentalize and ignore tragedy. It became part of my cholinergic response, fight or flight for me turning into file and reject in my memory bank.

The moment my husband came through the door relief washed over me. He was incredibly upset, but he was strong and his concern focused on my grief rather than his own. Together we listened to our multiple specialists as they explained our options. They were amazing and compassionate and shed many tears and prayed with me. And I can 100 per cent say that I received the best care following the accident.

The only options were to give birth naturally or have our baby removed surgically. I wanted to hold him and my husband wanted whatever the doctors suggested as best. I chose to give birth, but after some deliberation and hard decisions we decided to have the surgery instead. We were informed we could try in vitro again sooner with the four healthy embryos we had frozen by choosing the surgery.

I never got to see him, but I have a picture of his tiny hands and feet. A black and white 8x10 photo, a tiny finger and foot prints, and some ashes of the baby we never got to hold are all that remains. Our baby boy, my son's brother, would never meet his family. I can only imagine how my husband and son felt, my grief surpassing all ability to put myself in others' shoes. We were all mourning, and it wasn't my fault.

During this time, I'm in so much shock that I can barely comprehend what's going on. As I was wheeled back to have my son's body surgically removed, a hand grabbed mine. The same hand I used to steady during cheer routines and pyramid formations was now steadying my own. Her presence as my nurse meant more to me than I knew then. In great despair, I cried out to her, "I lost my boy."

Seeing her grounded my thoughts. She brought me back down to earth and with the realization, I accepted that the outside world could not be avoided. I'm not sure if I ever told her how grateful I was to have her there. So if she's reading this, thank you.

1st Memoir

Chapter 12

The first new house of my dreams

The day I was released from the hospital was also the day we moved into the new house. I remember walking in the door to a stunning mixed bouquet of white flowers wishing us well in our new home and sending sympathy for our loss at the same time. We had tons of help as I was unable to contribute. Still reeling and in pain from the accident while trying to stay in denial sent me into a dark place. I couldn't even go near the nursery. Trying to explain the loss of his brother to our four year old son was the hardest thing I had done up until that moment in my life. He didn't understand that mommy lost his brother in a car accident. My husband and I didn't understand it either.

My rescue dog was the rescuer here. He would (still does) stare at you with these large caring puppy dog eyes. He followed me everywhere, loving his new home and licked my tears as they flowed. I joked many times that my husband would pet him while sleeping, because this little rescue will nudge your hand over and over again, constantly petting himself. This little furbaby has become my son's favorite, and he claimed him as his own.

Trying to keep my mind occupied, I poured my heart into our new home. I built and designed and created. We experimented with paint colors and trim options. I learned about cathedral ceilings and air distribution, siding versus plank lap exteriors, 3-tab versus architectural shingles, the list goes on....

We planted trees and my husband had a beautiful swing built for the front porch. I picked out tile, granite and light fixtures and fell in love with the process. It was the only thing that gave me any feeling of accomplishment.

My husband was the same way, occupying himself building his dream vision in our backyard. He and Papa had a spacious metal garage built on the property before the bones of our house were constructed. He even had several small buildings set up, individual stations on our property, where he could perform different tasks and maintenance. This man was organized and had a plan!

We purchased a Kubota tractor in order to cut the grass on our large lot. It was a process that took hours but my husband loved that chore. And he loved grass, taking pride in landscaping by fertilizing and weeding regularly. He made sure to get the nicest model tractor, with audio and air conditioning so that our son could ride with him in comfort.

A fond memory recalls my husband, son, and I in our Polaris RZR sport side by side, riding the dirt roads next to the new house. My husband pulled over to the side of the road as a woman who lived behind us drove her car carefully past us. He immediately hailed her down, turning the RZR in her direction. He had noticed that one of her tires looked dangerously low. She was aware of it and on her way to get some air and to have it looked at. My husband would not allow her to proceed, not until she agreed to follow us back down our driveway so he could fill her tire. Her grandson was with her at the time, and he and our son played for a few minutes. She thanked my husband and offered to pay him, to which he politely, but unwaveringly, refused. He told her he only hoped someone would do the same for his wife and son. That's the kind of man he was. That's why we couldn't help but love him.

Over time life evened itself out. It was Christmas 2017, and we celebrated the holiday with happiness and love. We had each other and we knew we were blessed regardless of the struggles. The holiday was a favorite of ours, going all out with decorations and traditions and family gatherings. Our son was four and a half years old then, and the Christmas magic in our new dream home reached epic proportions.

The new year started and we were preparing for another cycle of IVF with one of the four remaining embryos. Feeling super confident this time, the stress was minimal and the excitement radio active.

Jan 25 changed that forever.

So.... As I'm sitting in my van racking my brain trying to figure out why I'm an adult being told to stay in my vehicle while on my own property... the woman informs me the sheriff is coming to talk to me. I'm finally allowed to get out of my van and prepare myself for the talk. I vividly remember giving them an unsure smile while walking towards them bracing myself. They verified that I was indeed the matriarch of the home with a few short questions before telling me anything, my anxiety and confusion increasing by the millisecond.

I had asked about my son. I had asked about the dogs. I asked if anyone working on the house had been hurt. When I pulled into the driveway I could've sworn I saw my husband running by the side of the house. In my side view I would've bet my life my husband, with his jeans and work boots, had sprinted around the corner of our home.

As I've said we had professionals and sub-contractors in and out of the yard and property all the time. Our three furbabies were constantly getting out due to open gates and my husband and I worried they would get hurt. We had discussed it the previous evening, and it was all my logical brain could find to explain the cause of such commotion.

The words the sheriff said took my breath away.

There's been an accident and your husband has been killed.

Wait, what?

No! No, my husband wasn't on the road that day, I said, to which the sheriff replied softly, the accident happened in the back yard.

Oh. My. God.

Chapter 13

This cannot be

Why is there no oxygen in the air?

Everything stopped. I wasn't able to comprehend, I couldn't react, couldn't inhale or exhale. I made eye contact with the woman, and the three officers. Their expressions were filled with sympathy and what I can only describe as authenticity.

They don't know what else to say. There's nothing else to say. They are waiting on me to respond, to absorb this information.

I can't blink and I'm staring face down at the ground. I don't remember bending over, but I'm about to fall. I'm not crying but tears are falling on the ground. I can barely see even though my immediate adrenaline release kept my eyes wide open. I literally cannot catch my breath.

At that moment my heart shattered. My brain was fighting the information I had

73

received while trying to find any logic. I was struggling to pull the oxygen out of the air surrounding me. I was fighting for answers. I was fighting to think, to move, to understand. I began pacing back and forth in the front yard. I'm stopped from going too far on either side of my home. And I'm told I cannot go inside as the accident happened in sight of our picturesque window overlooking the back half of our 10 acre property. I sit down on the ground. I get up and pace and scream to the top of my lungs. I lay down on the ground. Ants bite me. Everyone wants me to get up so I do and pace some more. Then I'm laying down again. I cannot stay still, cannot let the thoughts get through. My precious husband's life was taken tragically in the back of our dream home.

This can't be reality.

I cannot accept this to be true. I don't believe you. I don't believe you. I don't believe you....

The officers wanted me to call someone. Who could I call, my husband was gone. My mom had the flu, and my sister... I couldn't call her. Not after what she had been through. I couldn't do that to her. Through the confusion I opened my phone and called my friend who happens to be the best hairdresser (and therapist) on the planet, and a few minutes later she arrived at our home with the other amazing women she works with. They came to support me and I can only imagine what they saw when they pulled onto that same long gravel driveway. I'm so thankful that they were there in my state of instant grief....

The first ones on the scene with me, they reached out to our loved ones as I couldn't. I just couldn't. Over the next several hours until very late friends and family arrived in disbelief, by the dozens. So many people trying to make sense out of what happened, not having a clue how to. At one point a friend I hadn't seen in years appeared at my dining room table. Her face was a shock as I've since told her. It was at that moment I remember snapping into reality and my anger raged. I know I hit my hand on the cold granite kitchen island. I hit it several times out of pure desperation.

I'm not sure when I went to bed, but I do remember waking up to get a glass of water, my head splitting with a migraine and my hand throbbing. I saw my sister and husband's father sitting in my living room crying, and the sight stopped me dead in my tracks. In my sleepy grief riddled haze, it was the first of many painful reminders I was not having a nightmare. This was real.

The following days are so incredibly vivid and yet a complete blur. After the investigation it was determined my husband had been polishing his rims as he had done many times before. The sheriff concluded that the tractor trailer came off the jack he used to lift the rig and spin the wheels. It's assumed my husband was caught and trapped underneath. The guys (angels from above) working on the house had found him in the backyard earlier that morning and called 911.

I screamed. I cried.

This can't be reality.

Funeral arrangements, insurance policies, obituary. Flowers filling the house. Friends and family coming by to offer words of support. Their company and thoughtfulness appreciated but with each face, the reality tried to set in more.

The funeral was the most emotional experience of my life. When my father passed away, my husband remarked of the quality and quantity of attendees paying their respect. He said he could only hope to one day be that loved, and joked that he wouldn't have anyone at his funeral.

I can attest to the love and respect felt for my husband. So many family members, friends, and even strangers, came to honor his memory. I know for certain he was watching with pride and awe. I placed a written letter and a trinket in his pocket, our son's baby blanket, and the remaining ashes of our unborn son in the casket the evening before we laid him to rest. Everything went to fast, the theme of go, go, go, continued while I tried to thank each individual that went out of their way to share their sympathy. Again, it's all so vivid and yet an absolute blur.

My husband's best lifelong friend paid the most touching tribute. He knew my husband so well, and they spoke frequently about everything, religion in particular. He has a wealth of biblical knowledge and a level of understanding we can only aspire to. I still reach out to him and he has come to our rescue on more than one occasion.

My husband's fellow trucker best friend drove myself and my brother-in-law to the cemetery in my husband's black chromed out Peterbuilt, his 18-wheeler, with custom train horns. After the service he blew my husband's train horns he adored so much. In the graveyard, they echoed proudly as a goodbye tribute. It wasn't the last time we would hear those horns, thankfully. My husband's friend has them on his rig now, and we receive messages of those train horns still echoing through the mountains.

I would like to thank them both for honoring their best friend, my husband.

As inscribed on the back of my husband's tombstone, a modification of the poem,

A Trucker's Prayer

Lord help me to be safe as I

travel each mile. Let your presence guide me and bring me a smile.

Take care of my family while I am

away. Let them know I miss them

Each and every day.

After the emotional finality of the funeral, everyone followed to our new home, the home we hadn't yet lived six months in. I remember looking down and noticed I was wearing a navy blue dress with black leggings and black boots. At that moment I laughed out loud. My husband always picked on me for my slight issue with color blindness. I can see colors, please don't mistake my words, I just have a habit of mixing up dark navy and black. One of my Dogwoods had confirmed the dress was indeed black before I put it on. However, in the sunlight from that picturesque widow overlooking the back yard, the color was most definitely navy blue.

As everyone looked towards me in confusion, I explained my thoughts. The sound of combined laughter filled the house, and for them, was followed by a continuation of their conversations. But for me, reality hit again, and as the laughter faded, my tears returned.

The grieving widow, I went along with my role as best I could. All of these events are occurring and I'm functioning, but my brain refused to process the entirety of the situation....

I don't believe you. I don't believe you. I don't believe you.

The night of the accident, with my house brimming over with loved ones, I pulled my sister and cousin into my bedroom and sat on the spot where my husband slept. I told them that I feared for my sanity. My brain was doing everything it could to protect me but I felt like I was losing my mind.

I asked for help, I asked for company. At 38 years old, I had again lost the independence I had matured into. I asked to be babysat. I needed supervision just in case I couldn't snap out of the haze. Or my worst fear, snap all together.

I didn't see my son for two days following the accident. He had been affectionately cared for by a couple of angels in our lives, friends that my husband worked with and for. Their family had basically adopted my husband as one of their own. My son still recalls going to the lake with them and has fond memories of those two days.

So much was going on at the house including the investigation immediately following the accident, it wasn't the best environment for him to be in. The part that blew everyone's mind the most was that my husband's reputation for safety was unparalleled. He could haul anything, anywhere. Since he had been driving his entire adult life, he knew his job and he knew his rig. And he was insistent that our son stay a great distance away from his equipment while playing and riding his custom toys in the yard. He didn't cut corners when it came to safety around those massive trucks. It didn't make any sense, and somewhere deep inside me I had a glimmer of hope they would tell me they were mistaken, and that my husband was still alive.

Although I missed my son terribly, I dreaded the moment he would have to return home. With two days to think about it, I prepared myself to tell my son his father was dead. I couldn't stop this reality from affecting him no matter how sad or angry or accepting I was. Our lives were forever altered, unimaginably.

What do I say, how do I tell him...

When my son came home and walked in the door, he was happy to see me but confusion and curiosity filled his face. The house was still overflowing with people who were helping the best they could. With a tremendous amount of willpower I looked my son in his beautiful blue eyes, and I told him his father had gone to heaven to be with his brother. He was four and a half years old then and didn't understand that he would never see his dad again. He didn't understand he would never be a big brother. We were all trying to understand it.

He didn't cry, didn't comprehend the magnitude of reality. He asked questions that I couldn't answer. I still can't answer most of them. I have tried many times to see from his point of view and understand the way he must've felt. We had gone from a family of almost four to a family of two.

My heart broke over my loss, but the pain and anguish I felt from my son's perspective was debilitating. He was so young but remembers events and memories we shared while his father was alive. From the very first home we lived in, the pool, the frog, the neighbors, he remembers so much from those early years. And he remembers the future we had planned.

Thank goodness for cameras on phones, and we're blessed with so many videos and candid shots with my husband in them. We had been active as a young family, visiting Disney on three separate vacations. In the year 2014, we bought a yellow deck boat, a Hurricane, that we all enjoyed, even our two furbabies, and I have treasured memories from the lake days. We frequented fun parks, fairs, and festivals, and went on beach trips with our cousins. Truly every photo, most especially the candid ones, are beyond priceless. Whether we were out and about doing something crazy fun or miserably boring, or at home chilling being lazy or productive, I value each one of my photos equally.

Over the next six months my son and I experienced a mind blowing amount of support from friends, family and strangers. We were never alone and I can tell you their presence kept my sanity intact as much as possible. There were calendars and sign-up sheets and so many people took the time to share their company with my son and I. I still have the calendars and all the notes from those months.

My Dogwoods and my family showed up and took over. They took the lead and the heavy weight of reality off of my shoulders as much as they could. My sister and cousin, being the super-women that they are, took over organizing the funeral arrangements and my Dogwoods took charge of my home.

My sister and cousin went to the funeral home and began the preparations according to my wishes. From the choices I was presented with, I selected a sleek black casket with chrome accents. The vault top was an easy pick, choosing the same diamond plating my husband decked his trucks out in. The flowers were similar to our wedding, with orchids highlighting the purple theme. The Dogwood that sang to honor our wedding sang again to honor my husband's life, with the same pastor who joined our hands together before God in 2010. I wanted his clothing to represent him, not what everyone expected. So I approved his favorite ragged jeans and trucking LLC work shirt for the service.

And my Dogwoods showed me what true friendship really means. Greeting visitors, talking with me, keeping me company, helping gather photos and memories, enduring my heartbreak as their own. Checking on my facility, encouraging me to eat and drink, cleaning up anything they could find, sticking with me during the hardest moments of my life, they became my caregivers and held the broken pieces of my heart together.

Weeks at a time, leaving their own families, they selflessly offered me their strength and support. I can honestly say these women could rule the world. But as time passed, watching over me was taking its toll on my loved ones.

So my sister came up with the best solution, and a dear friend agreed to live with my son and I. She was my therapy, listening and talking when needed. Laughing and crying sometimes back to back, her youthful energy and perspective brought some of the pieces of myself I had long stop caring for back to life. Thanks to her for being the glue that kept me from floating away as the earth kept revolving....

This outpouring of kindness reached the depths of my soul. Because of the bond shared between us, and for the love they had for my son and husband, everyday human beings became our personal superheroes.

I continued functioning on auto pilot, tending to my son but never feeling present. I couldn't focus enough to drive so my support system took care of me. They drove us to and from my son's school every morning and afternoon. They drove me to do my job. They helped me add figures and keep track of the business I owned. My son had been part of the local basketball program when That Day happened, and with their assistance, he finished the season. I was there for every game and practice. When my son's team learned about the accident they made him a themed basket of trinkets and goodies. And love, it was a basket of love.

My family, probate lawyer, and our wonderful accountant helped with the estate and dissolving my husband's company. I'm truly thankful for so much support and assistance with all the legality and formality following my husband's death. And I must compliment my husband's book keeping skills. His paperwork was immaculate and so easy to understand.

This genuine support meant as much to me then as it does to this day. So to all of them, including our neighbor that helped get our furbabies to the groomer, thank you from the bottom of my heart.

One of the best memories I have with my Dogwoods happened that summer, July 8th, 2018. The four of us had floor seats at The Imagine Dragons Evolve World Tour. I had become a huge fan of the group before my husband's accident, and he insisted we go when they toured. My three Dogwoods and I attended the concert together in his honor, five days after my 39th birthday. It was the best concert of my life. At that point anyway....

1st Memoir

Chapter 14

Identity lost

Is there a purpose to life? I hope that there is. What is my purpose? Who am I now?

My obsession with growing our family died with my husband. The past seven years of my life had been consumed with treating my body like a temple. I was the epitome of health. My identity revolved around my family, and the loss of my purpose was replaced immediately with insurmountable grief. The overwhelming waves of the initial stages brought two friends' guilt and anxiety along and planted roots in my thoughts. Survivors guilt. Fear of losing my mind. Feelings of anger. Feelings of inadequacy. Feelings of panic and loss of control.

Was I being punished for being greedy. Did my obsession with IVF cost me my unborn son and husband? Was I not meant to put attitude and effort into growing my family? Did wanting more result in having less? Did I just cause my son's loss of his father in the process of trying to give him a sibling? These thoughts cross my mind every day still....

I couldn't process the accident. It was too much. I had to survive and that meant protecting my mental state as much as possible. Most everyone knows the five stages of grief: denial, anger, bargaining, depression, and acceptance. My body, my mind refused to do the last stage. So part of me stayed numb and oblivious that my husband and son's father was really truly gone. Every time I thought about the things we would miss, the events he wouldn't be present for, all the roles he wanted to fill in his son's life...I just couldn't.

I don't want to believe you.

Time went by. The fog in my head remained but the world kept spinning. Somewhere, somehow I came across the information that my mom had cancer, Stage IV, and she had been sick since before my husband's accident. She had been sick for a very long time.

Wait, what?

How could my family not tell me? I worked with my mother and saw her almost daily. How did I not notice?

Within months my mom moved into our home as she couldn't care for herself. I witnessed her suffer and struggle trying to eat and drink, not knowing how far her cancer had progressed. Thinking she was going to get fluids and IV nutrition, she wound up admitted to the hospital and never improved. New scans revealed the disease had spread just about everywhere. She suffered at the end and my desire for her to get better changed. I wanted her to go, to find peace and relief. My sister and I told her we would be ok and to let go. Whether she heard us or not, we will never know. She died Oct 1st, 2018, the same year as my husband. Funeral arrangements, insurance policies, obituary. My mother, my friend, and my son's grandmother, gone just like that.

This can't be reality...

As I've said, I couldn't process my grief. So I used every vice I could find to escape reality. I made many bad decisions in the years after my husband's accident. Although I had good intentions, my fog, also referred to as widow's brain, caused me to miss important moments, procrastinate on projects, make poor decisions, and put me in a general state of constant anxiety.

I have no idea how to explain the feeling. It's a never ending state of panic and unease. It's the inability to get comfortable. It's fear, of the unknown and loss of control. It's watching your dreams magically disappear without having a part in the smoke and mirrors show. Because that's what it felt like, a show. I felt like I was living a poorly scripted drama show. As I've said many times, and still to this day, the candid camera guy can come out at any time now. This show isn't funny.

Before I sold the facility I met a guy. We got married. My five year old son called him dad. That's the single biggest regret of my entire life.

Chapter 15

The second home of my dreams

The huge fog of grief refused to clear. The world kept turning and I kept on fighting to find my balance. However it was clear to me that I couldn't continue as an administrator or caregiver anymore. As I've said before, the facility was a wonderful environment full of love and I considered the residents my family. But it's tough to form bonds with people at the end stages of life. Many of them eventually passed away at the facility or hospital, or they moved to a more skilled nursing facility. Health care, especially hospice or end of life care, demands strength and a security in yourself that I didn't possess at the time. The residents and staff deserved an owner-administrator that cared about them and the facility. And during that time I only cared about one thing. Surviving, for my son and furbabies, was my only priority.

There was only one option available. I made the difficult choice to move on from the facility my grandmother started. I had spent 41 years of my life in that environment. I still hear from them every now and then to this day. As I've said, we are family.

After selling the Assisted Living Facility I purchased a tanning salon. Yep, big change! I know. And it was exactly what I needed!

The salon was a sign, a gift from up above. I was at a hairdresser (therapy) appointment telling my friend my goals. They included moving on from the facility and opening a salon in a different city. The words she said took my breath away.

"You know the tanning salon across the street is for sale".

Sitting in that same chair that my son and husband had also sat in many times, it was an arrow pointing me in the right direction.

The salon provided my son and I a second home base that brought out more of both of our creative sides. It was something totally new to me, and I loved it. The energy and vibe of the clientele contrasted sharply with the facility's requirements, and my son and I fed off their positivity.

And my employees were the absolute best. Their friendship was an unexpected bonus in such a positive way that I didn't see coming. I valued each one of my girls, and one young woman went above and beyond to show me true kindness on my 42nd birthday. My now ex husband made me miserable, which was typical behavior during any celebration or holiday or special event.

My angel of an employee went out of her way to decorate the salon and even had a cake and birthday candles, a 4 and a 2. I laughed saying you didn't have to get the actual numbers 42. She didn't miss a beat and flipped the numbers to 24. I laughed so hard my tears of appreciation changed to tears of absolute enjoyment, her comedic timing being on point. This young woman, welcoming us as if we were indeed her family, was another gift from up above. Including us in birthday celebrations and holidays and showing up when it mattered, she quickly worked her way into my son's and my heart. She grounded me with her logic and reasoning. And during my miserable second marriage I needed all the rationality I could get. She also deserves the credit for finding my son's passion of stop-motion film making. At a very young age she had inspired both of us. And to this day her family comprises some of our favorite people. I'm so eternally grateful for the woman that she is, and for their continued presence in our lives.

I have to take a moment to appreciate everyone I met through the salon!

Thank you for sharing that adventure with me! Those were some of the best years because of you all!

Even through the fog I also realized we couldn't remain in the home where the accident happened. Picking up my phone I called our realtor yet again, and with great determination I decided to build another home.

Finding the perfect lot seemed impossible seeing as how I felt we were already in it. However a hidden gem, a heavily wooded deep lot backing up to the golf course, had been waiting for someone to notice its potential. I made an offer that was accepted on a lot that had been listed for many years. I later learned two other offers came in within days after mine was contingent.

Same amazing contractor, but this time the project was mine and mine alone. I devoted my life to this second new house of my dreams. It didn't take long to find my ideal home plans, and before I knew it, we were cutting down trees and adding water access.

As the structure began, the bones revealed tall ceilings, 11 foot to be exact. I vividly remember walking into the framed structure thinking, good lord the ceiling is so high. My contractor informed me we would need taller doors than standard sizes, and from there my ideas skyrocketed. When I walked into the master closet, I had to ask what the room was. With its two-story ceiling, the enormous space didn't look like any closet I had ever seen. Similar to a wedding dress, the bigger the closet, the bigger the possibilities. Or as my first husband and father would've said, go big or go home.

As the process of selling and buying and moving is complicated, my son and I left the first home we had built and pulled into our brand new driveway on a Thursday evening in November, 2020. Because of closing dates we moved into our home before it was completely finished. It was habitable and safe, as we had the letter of occupancy approval, just not completed.

I remember spending the first night in our new home with mattresses on the floor. I had to peel the packing tape off the tub to give my son a bath. It was like camping. And looking back it was great. It was as if we had front row tickets to a beautiful symphony, and the contractors made up the orchestra.

It was an experience I will never forget, but also a pivotal moment in my journey with grief. It became an outlet for my expression, and a form of therapy for me. I became obsessed with design, watching first hand as the 11 foot ceilings and large space with custom size interior doors and custom farmhouse crown molding were placed into position. Seeing the tile accents and backsplashes installed, and my favorite paint color Naval (Sherwin Williams 2020 color of the year) highlight cabinets and shiplap, I found it extremely satisfying to witness. My bold wallpaper accents accentuated the large spaces in the home, even in the master closet. I couldn't have a two story closet without a moveable library ladder for easy access now could I? My contractor said sure, he could build one of those. This contractor and his sub contractors were at the top of their game. And this house was over the top.

I can say the closet was my second favorite space in the home. My most favorite being the enormous screened in back porch with custom pull down privacy shades and natural gas stone fireplace. Many wonderful and enlightening conversations happened on that porch, many bonds both formed and broken. With an irrigation system and exterior lit front and back yard, my perfectly planned landscaping set off the unique angles of the home. A 1.4 acre lot overlooking the golf course, it was the property of my dreams. My masterpiece.

Being present and making decisions as the crew worked together on the house, was like watching tiny roots developing into a massive tree. But it was my tree, my roots. I was creating and it became my passion. And I learned so many valuable lessons during the process of building those two homes. I'm eternally grateful to all those involved in both projects! Everyone I worked with, and since I built the two homes with the same amazing individuals, I got to know about their lives and their families. I had learned early on from my facility days when people randomly talk to you about something, whether important or not, there's always a lesson, a message coming through.

So I absorbed their knowledge like a sponge and I consider them a part of our family too. To this day our amazing contractor still reaches out with support and words of encouragement, generally a perfect bible verse that fits many different scenarios. He is a good man, the co-captain with his beautiful wife, of a an incredible family brimming with integrity. And we think the world of them. So did my first husband. And my son will tell you that there isn't anything our contractor can't build. Because there isn't.

Seeing my designs coming together gave me a feeling of accomplishment I hadn't felt since losing my son and since my reality started shredding strand by strand. It healed me in ways I didn't see coming, you know, in a good way.

Chapter 16

Not the best man I'll ever meet

That's when I began to realize the guy I married was not the man he pretended to be. Everyone had warned me that I was making a mistake, even my first husband's father stopped visiting us. But while I was vulnerable, he was an opportunist. I had written specific grievances in the first drafts of this book detailing the events but came to realize it's not worth the space. Not in this memoir. The subtitle is a journey though love and loss. My second marriage was neither of those things.

The take-away is, I refused to live a miserable existence being verbally, emotionally, and financially abused. My first husband taught me what love and family are all about. My second husband taught me what love and family most definitely are not.

My son and I had discussed his little brother's and father's death many times since

That Day, in therapy and in general. As I've said there are some things I still can't explain and there are details that haven't been revealed at his young age.

And there are things he knows that I'm not aware of in regards to his perspective. I can say that he and I have openly and extensively discussed my second marriage, and all of the events following the accident. I am aware of his feelings as much as he is willing to allow. But his feelings are not mine to share.

After the loss of our unborn son in 2017, I began to see a therapist for my grief. My sessions increased after my husband's accident and our son began visits with her as well. With our psychologists we are both still navigating the five stages of grief as best we can.

COVID hit during this version of myself. It was also during this time that my best friend passed away from cancer. It was Jan 23, 2021 when we said goodbye to her. While the other Dogwoods went to see her one last time, I said goodbye over FaceTime. The other Dogwoods held the phone so I could be there in some manner. I had tested positive for COVID and couldn't spread the virus. Not only was I positive, I had major flu like symptoms. That was a very hard January.

Watching her suffer, wishing she would improve changed to wishing she would die. She put up an amazing fight being so young, but her cancer progressed rapidly. She was in pain long before she was even properly diagnosed. And when she realized the severity of her prognosis she worried about her son and husband, and how they would survive without her.

Saying goodbye to my best friend via video chat, watching her in her last moments, her beautiful soul in agony, it was flipping messed up. I mourned the day she died and the grieving continued two days later for the anniversary of my first husband's death. January is a month that will always be grey and dark in my world.

It made no sense that she was dying in front of our eyes when she had so much love to share with her family and with the world. Just like when my mother died, we wanted her to be at peace, she deserved that much.

I was honored to be a bridesmaid in her wedding, and she was my Maid of Honor in mine. An amazing person, she looked at the world and saw kindness everywhere because she was full of positivity. She wasn't perfect or innocent. But she was the purest person I've ever known, her intentions always genuine. Determination and her strong belief in God shaped her personality. She saw hope and good in the world. I trusted her completely and she felt the same for me. A daughter, sister, wife, mother, and friend, her most valued role was mother. Her son's presence on this earth is also another miracle story that's not mine to share. However, I can tell you that he has grown from an adorable child to a handsome young man, with distinctive qualities from both his parents. An amazing kid, he is also best friends with my son. Knowing she was leaving him weighed heavily on us all, unimaginably so on her. She fought cancer with every ounce of strength and faith she had. And she overflowed with both qualities.

It was on her wedding day in 2017 that the OG Dogwood had the aneurysm. She had become the fourth Dogwood, lovingly filling the role while honoring the OG. And now we were attending her funeral, another loss of someone we truly genuinely loved. Her miracle child now without his mother, and her husband, a widower.

<u>In her honor, please be aware that colon cancer is the one of the most preventable forms there is. Get checked. Get checked before they recommend it if you're experiencing unexplained and unresolved pain.</u>

<u>That goes for any pain and specialist.</u>

Before she passed we had agreed to get Dogwood tattoos together. It was her idea, but we all wanted to honor our bond. She never improved enough to get inked, but the three of us did with the image she picked out. Out of all of the things I wear - clothing, jewelry, perfume, it's the most valuable item on me. And being on my inside wrist I always catch a glimpse of it during activities of daily living. Makes me smile every time. Every single time!

The three remaining Dogwoods and I send pictures of our tattoos frequently to each other as a way to say, I'm thinking of you, or it's been a hard day, or it's been a fabulous day. Sharing that image among us three can mean one of those things or all of them. It's a code, a special symbol we send to offer and receive support. Whenever one sends the image, the other two always send one in return. It's a beautiful testament to our connection and genuine friendship.

As time went on the fog clouding my thoughts began to clear. The new house and salon gave me renewed purpose and I was finding happiness again. That did not sit well with my second husband or his family. As I became less vulnerable and more aware my second marriage came into focus. This new transparency opened my eyes to behaviors I could no longer ignore and actions I could no longer tolerate. I was anxious and edgy around him, my son and I frequently staying later than needed at the salon. It was peaceful there.

Meanwhile the home of my dreams had become filled with unfounded anger and resentment. I was miserable and cried all the time. I decided some changes had to be made. I realized my son was living my life as a child, watching my second husband and I argue. He accepted his mommy crying as normal. It's because of my son that I found the strength to make the necessary changes.

I began to say no to my second husband and his family. I cut off everything being provided that wasn't reciprocated. I no longer supported him in ways he never supported me. Throughout our relationship, I was the provider for everyone and everything.

The breaking point was when I caught him in a lie. I caught him, and he denied it. His friends and family accused me of being in the wrong. His mother and daughters excusing his every action, no matter what he did, it was always my fault, my responsibility, my problems. Even their problems were my problems. Never in my life have I met such unimaginably entitled people. After counseling and promising I'll make it up to you with changed behavior, I had a glimmer of hope our marriage was salvageable. He did change, however, it wasn't an improvement.

And he told me over and over I would never meet a better man than him.

This version of myself I did not care for. After learning that everyone I had associated with during my second marriage used myself and my son, I burned bridges that shouldn't have been standing to begin with. Those people weren't my friends, they didn't care about my son. They just hung around for the benefits. I cut everyone off with the word 'no', this will not be my reality.

The only positive from my second marriage was a little dog my son and I had fallen in love with. Enter furbaby number four... he's a tiny lovely little guy and all four of our furbabies love each other, his best friend being our rescue. He has the best temperament of any dog I've ever loved. Smart, sweet, and absolutely adorable, he was our baby, and I fought for him in the divorce. No family member of ours gets left behind.

I also fought for a house full of furniture belonging to my family, what was left of it anyway. My late brother-in-law's curio cabinet, my mother's antique entryway table, and the bedroom set my first husband and I purchased together are still in my second husband's home, along with various other heirlooms. And even though I could've sued for the amount of the furnishings, I chose to let him keep them. After picking up the things he did provide, I shut that door and never looked back.

Though I chose the separation, the ensuing legal battle broke my heart, again. When I asked my ex to leave our family home during the beginning of our separation, I felt bad. My son didn't want to speak to him, like not at all. I felt so sad for my now ex being alone without his family, missing out on the fun moments and routines. Missing our evening prayers...

My ex husband moved out of my home November 29th, 2021. My son and I spent that first Christmas morning completely alone. It was difficult to get into the spirit that year. My son had a fabulous holiday, although different, he was still thrilled. With Jan 22nd approaching, the first anniversary of our beloved Dogwood's passing, and That Day of my husband's accident Jan 25th back to back, I prepared myself to face these days on my own.

However it proved to be impossible and I picked up my phone to call my second husband. I reached out for support. I reached out for friendship. I reached out because I was in pain, and at that time I thought we were amicable.

It was on the anniversary of That Day, he informed me he had found something special with someone else. Only separated two months, while sitting in my two story master closet on speaker phone with my son within earshot, my second marriage died.

At one point I fell to my knees on my back porch and begged for help, for God to pick me up, for my first husband's strength to lift me.

And I was heard.

I will always carry the regret of my second marriage. I will always be ashamed of myself for the person I was, my choices, my actions, my thoughts. This specific moment of disbelief in reality was caused by me. There was nothing to figure out, no trying to make sense out of tragedy. It was just stupid. I was stupid. It was my fault I married him. It was my fault I allowed their dull knives to wound me repeatedly in my most vulnerable spots. I made many mistakes after my first husband lost his life. It was his accident, but I was left wrecked.

I will never forgive myself for being that version. It would invalidate the trauma I allowed to happen. And I know my son's father was looking down with such disappointment.

It's still so hard to believe...again,

This can't be reality....

February 12, 2022 the two Dogwoods and I attended our second Imagine Dragons concert. We had floor VIP tickets for their Mercury Tour and it was an amazing and emotional experience! Their lyrical stories expressing our emotions, caught up in the magic and music, it was like I was home for the first time in a very long time. We honored our missing Dogwood's memory by bringing pieces of her with us. Her bracelet, the one that matched ours, is in the pictures we took.

Being recently separated and going through the divorce, while simultaneously grieving the loss of so many loved ones, their music broke me down and built me back up. If you've never been to an Imagine Dragons' concert or listened to their music, I highly suggest checking them out. Their second show was the best concert of my life. So far anyway....

1st Memoir

Chapter 17

Standing on my own feet

My son and I were living in our second custom built home. A home we loved and the home that saved me. By bringing my vision into existence, I was able to find pieces of myself again, some that I didn't even know existed. But it was a miserable home void of peace and happiness. So I made the difficult decision to leave it all behind and start over. Again.

My mom had been the glue holding us there, and my son's Papa wouldn't even respond when I sent him pictures and videos of his grandson on his cellphone. A phone line that I paid for. I haven't heard from Papa in five years now. To this day, my son will occasionally ask if his Papa is still alive. "I'm not sure baby," is always my response. Because, technically, I have no clue. Last thing I heard about my son's grandfather he was living his life, happy and healthy. He was and is still independent in activities of daily living. I never actually understood what his disability really was. I still don't understand why he never reached back out to us, but I have a strong feeling it's over money. As my son's only living grandparent, he abandoned us. He abandoned his only family, as my late husband was his only child. And as far as I'm concerned, he can stay abandoned.

At my son's 3rd grade end of the year awards ceremony, we learned several of his favorite instructors would no longer be working at the school. As much as they loved their positions on the campus, they made difficult decisions that led them in other directions. My son and I were both disappointed with the information but happy for each of them for pursuing their dreams.

That awards ceremony inspired me though, and that very weekend I began looking at school options and real estate in various locations. All of our homes had been in my hometown, but with our situation, the possibilities were endless. After talking through the idea with my sister, she supported the possible change. And her opinion had always meant the world to me, always will.

Discussing it with my son did not go as well as with my sister. He was not thrilled with the plan, not at first anyway. We were both tired of moving and were in love with our home, our sanctuary, my masterpiece. But as time went on, we both thought about it more, and found ourselves enjoying debating the pros and cons. One day we realized the pros side was infinitely larger than the cons column. We accepted that change would be hard but looked at the opportunities instead of the obstacles. A brand new start appealed more and more and both of us found excitement again. Once we had made our minds up, I continued with the process of getting my masterpiece home inspected, appraised, photographed, and listed.

As things began to transpire at the beginning of that summer, the process was extremely smooth and what I would call easy. Everything just *kinda* flowed from there. The idea caught traction and took off on its own. Calling our amazing realtor again, she didn't miss a beat. Her response being a simple, "Ok, where we going this time?" I adored her, and with her assistance, I trusted the process. Before I knew it, my son was enrolled in a new school and I had contingent offers on both our current masterpiece home and our new dream home. Everything happened so fast that we started packing immediately and still required major assistance moving.

I'm not joking about the major assistance needed, and the guys that helped my son and I organize and load must've been sent from Heaven above. They kept repeating, "We've got you ma'am, stop worrying." And you know what, they sure did. They came to my rescue a second time as well, but again, that's not the subject for this particular memoir.

Our relocation also meant leaving the salon I purchased after selling the facility. So much loss so fast had left me feeling like a machine. I loved my salon like I loved my home. But I turned it off, flipped the switch, and just like I had made the impossibly difficult decision to leave the facility my grandmother created, I made the same difficult choice with the salon. I left two beautiful homes that I designed from the ground up. We just left it all behind.

Although my son and I toured different schools in different locations all over the state, my heart was set on one destination, on one neighborhood in particular. There are four main reasons why we focused on such a narrow property search.

1. One reason is because of the public school system. The elementary school is

one of the best in our state. Coming from an incredible smaller private school, my Alma Mater, my son and I both were reluctant to leave that environment and family atmosphere. But after researching the amenities and programs at length over and over, I decided the move and new location would be the best choice for our family. My son now has access to more programs and services than a private school could provide. This school is how all public schools should be. The neighborhood highly sought after because of this and for many other amazing reasons.

2. The second appeal to this area was because one of my Dogwoods had resided there in a gorgeous home for over a decade with her family. My son and I had visited her huge but quaint neighborhood many times for sleepovers and pool days. And we loved everything about it.

3. The third main attraction that drew us to our new location is hard to summarize. We live in an area that is big without being excessive yet small without being limiting. The landscape

has oak trees and ponds and sidewalks and trails. It's like being in the country with some of the hidden areas in our golf course community. However we're close to a major city full of programs my son has interest in. Programs that weren't available in our home town.

4. And lastly, the area is perfect for the salon I intend to open. It's at the top of my personal goals list. I really truly loved everything about the vibe, and miss the positive energy very much. My salon, Luminosity, will offer cosmetology services along with esthetics featuring UV hybrid and UV free tanning options. In addition, but not limited to, the newest Ergoline Equipment and, specifically the total immersion hydro jet massage therapy bed. I hope to open it as soon as I locate the ideal spot I envision, its home base being critical for my selection.

Really every single thing about the lifestyle we visited appealed to us on so many different levels. Even the traffic didn't and still doesn't bother me. Being in a new location was intimidating, but knowing a Dogwood was a golf cart ride away brought a sense of security

I didn't see coming, you know, in a very much needed and appreciated way.

Moving is always stressful. You would think by that point I would have mastered the art of relocating, but I was at the time going through what I can only call a ridiculous divorce. I wish I could say the transition was smooth, but that wouldn't go with the story.

During the purchase of our fourth new home, I could not proceed without a verification statement from my estranged second husband. The statement required his agreement that he had no intent to contest the prenup. Our prenup stated we kept our property separate, and his name wasn't on the deed or title of my home or golf course property. We had a solid prenuptial agreement. My real estate lawyer confirmed this, at the same time telling me I still needed the verification letter.

I still don't understand why the letter was needed. What's the point of a prenup if it has to be verified? Considering he purposely delayed the divorce hearing, my July 22nd divorce date turned into September 22nd. The divorce should've been history by the time we moved. But once he learned the letter was needed, the manipulation started all over again. He stated in an email to my lawyer that he did contest the prenup because he was unhappy with the terms of his at fault divorce agreement. He demanded remediation and refused to retain a lawyer. (Remediation is not even the correct term for this situation.) It was the day before closing, after I had informed my real estate agents that the sales could not legally continue, that my ex agreed to provide the letter. This was only after my divorce attorney threatened a secondary substantial loss lawsuit, in addition to our family court proceedings.

I can't explain the turmoil this simple letter caused for my logical brain. However, I knew I was on the correct path. There were signs everywhere guiding me. One of these signs occurred through a friend of my first husband, whom I hadn't spoken to since his funeral. Seeing her name on my caller ID forced the air from my lungs again. Hesitantly I answered and, with excitement lacing her voice, she informed me that my masterpiece home had an offer less than 24 hours after listing, for the full asking price, sight unseen! This friend and associate that I knew mostly through my husband, felt compelled to call and share the good news with me. As I spoke with her tears of relief fell from my eyes.

But the tears were not only of overwhelming surprise and happiness. That phone call happened to be on my first husband's birthday. On the back porch, the same place where I had fallen to my knees, my husband was sending me a message through her. A woman who has known tremendous loss herself, unwittingly communicated to me his love, support and guidance. It was a moment I will never forget. I realized then that my husband hadn't stopped looking out for his family. I just hadn't been paying attention. With renewed confidence, I felt I was finally making the right decisions, finally moving in the right direction on our journey to start over! Signs....

Again, moving is hard and although I had support, I was all alone. The only one responsible. The only adult. The only one that my son had to turn to. The only disciplinarian. The only comforter. The only one to make important decisions. It was and still is, a heavy weight to bear.

During this adjustment my then eight yr old son was absolutely amazing. We had renovators in and out of the house for 32 days. 32 days of renovations gone awry. My anxiety was high and I had no control over my environment. Things kept being moved and our furbabies and I were stressed to the max. But my son kept on trucking and being himself. His calmness and quick acclimation to our new environment both impressed and inspired me.

And with his positive influence I began to relax and settle in. The next few months flew by. I had become comfortable in our new location and my son was thriving. The home we now call our own isn't exactly my ideal choice, as I didn't build it. But considering the location and lot, I probably would have. It's a two story home which I've never been a fan of. But the large open floor plan suits our needs better than even I predicted, and even better than our previous homes. Our little piece of paradise turned out to be literal paradise. The home, neighborhood, and school district provided much more than I had anticipated, and I had high hopes starting out.

Conclusion

Foreverville

This is the part of the story where I can say everything was perfect. Or is perfect - present tense - to be exact!

I'm happy again. Like really truly happy! The neighborhood we live in is picture perfect. Our surroundings are ideal for our needs. The houses to my left and to my right are inhabited by the most amazing people and I get to call them not only neighbors but friends. Everyone here looks out for each other, and unbeknownst to them I've added another family to our crew. The foreverville family....

My son beams and adores his life. He has been involved in a variety of extracurricular activities, and his passion remains still film making. In our movie like, surreal, too good to be true setting, we walk on a path in the morning and afternoons to and from his amazing school. We hold hands and chat, smelling the flowers when blooming or holding a flashlight on those dark fall mornings. The other walkers on the path say good morning and happy whatever day of the week it is. Their friendly greetings providing the positive energy that fuels and begins our day.

He has made many friends that we both adore, and he has this funny yet caring disposition about him. Throughout everything my son has experienced in his young lifetime, he has remained resilient with understanding and compassion. He's maturing and growing and getting tall and handsome like his father. He is so much like his dad, same silly humor, same taste in music, same nose, same mesmerizing blue eyes. And I am truly honored with the privilege of being his No 1 Fan.

It has taken longer than expected to open my salon, but life doesn't always go as planned as I've learned repeatedly. In the meantime, I'm enjoying my son being the center of my world. He just turned 11 yrs old, just started 5th grade.

We've been in our piece of Heaven for two years now. It's all so amazing and mind blowing and the world is revolving exponentially faster and faster, moment by moment, and I'm standing still watching it rotate on its axis in awe....

Wait, what?

Yes I am in awe. Didn't see that one coming, but I am enamored with my life. I am grateful for what I have and what I've had. I'm becoming who I was meant to be, comfortable in my own skin.

There's peace in my heart, in my son's heart, and in our home. There's pride in myself, for my son, and even regarding our furbabies. We have all survived many huge storms and adapted with every obstacle thrown our way. There's genuine unconditional love shared between my son and I, and between the circle I am honored to have. There's beauty in the world and I see potential everywhere.

I've built and reinvented myself so many times, I've lost count. And I know I will again, because perspectives change every day. With each experience we view the world a little differently.

But that's the beauty of life, we constantly adapt. We evolve every moment we learn or unlearn something new or something alters our reality. Perception is everything, and the way we view the world controls our opinions and the choices we make.

I choose to see the beauty along with the pain. I choose to see treasure where others would see trash. I choose to see perfection in the flawed.

Because in my opinion nothing is ever perfect.

And that's reality.

I continue to miss the loves I've lost. I will always mourn their absence. And there will be more loss. My oldest furbaby is 15 at the moment I'm writing this. She was the first baby of our family and has been with me through it all. She's a happy feisty little thing still, but when the time comes my heart will hurt and tears will fall. And more pieces of who I am will end. And I will miss her for the rest of my life. I know I will say goodbye for the last time with each of the four we love so deeply. Loving them is easy, losing them will be hard.

And my son will continue to mature and our relationship will change. We have always been close so when the time comes for him to start driving and dating and living his own life, I will mourn the previous stages. But, I will also appreciate the man he's becoming, just as I do the young man he's already become.

And....I am aging. At 45, I'm wiser and stronger than I've been at any other point in my life. But with great power comes great responsibility, or so my son's favorite superhero seems to think. In my case my wisdom has come at the price of my youth, and the challenges that lie ahead I cannot begin to imagine. But I embrace them because I love the person I've become. I love the person I'm still becoming. And I now know my loved ones are watching from above feeling pride. And relief. An enormous amount of relief.

I've lived through love and loss. I've adapted over and over again. I've restarted so many times when my identity was stripped from me.

So I try not to worry about the future, don't dwell on the past, and I try to live in the present. My elevens are always gonna hurt, but we have what I consider perfection, peace and happiness in the place we lay our heads and in our hearts. And I'm enjoying my life again. Right at this moment, everything is as it should be.

Wait, what?

Is this reality?

Yes. Yes, it is real. I have moments of joy again, real pure joy. I totally didn't see that coming.

Is there a purpose to life?

If so, what's mine? What's the end game?

It's taken every moment of my 45 years to gain the perspectives I have, and my takeaway is gratitude. Through all that life has thrown my way, I'm a survivor. My son is a survivor. And I am grateful to be alive.

I will continue to question everything, and that's never going to change. The ability to let go while retaining the lessons learned is a fine line to tread, and I lose my balance quite often. But I have enormous appreciation for the highs while expecting the inevitable lows. Because they are both inevitable. The point is to live...to live through them all.

And I can't wait to see what happens next.

Thanks to everyone I've mentioned on these pages: My sister, my Dogwoods, family, friends, and strangers alike, thanks for the support and genuine concern.

Thanks to Michael for giving me the patience and understanding I needed while reliving these experiences and encouraging me to share them.

Congratulations on your book,

Two Days on a Calendar!

And

Thanks to

Imagine Dragons

for every song they've ever released, especially Wrecked.

A photographic journey through love and loss
can be found on the following platforms:

Facebook

This Cant Be Reality

Jimilyn Smith Kell

Instagram

@thiscantbereality

@JimilynSmithKell

TikTok

@realitymemoirs

@JimilynSmithKell

YouTube

@realitymemoirs

www.ingramcontent.com/pod-product-compliance
Lightning Source LLC
Chambersburg PA
CBHW071156120626
46546CB00006B/2293